D1371314

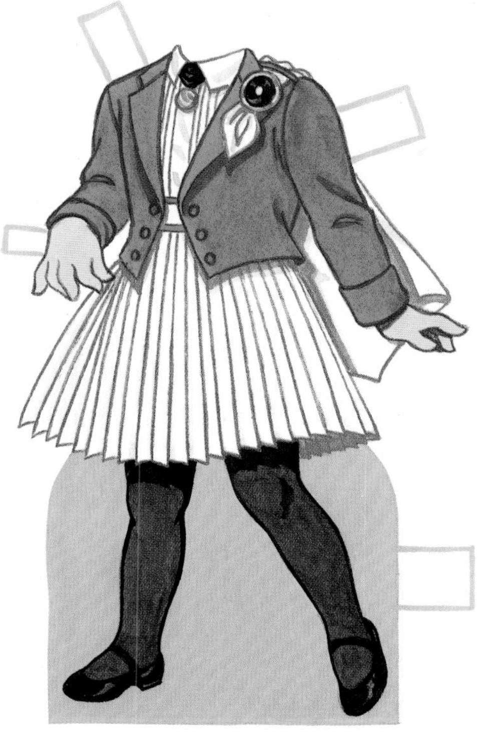

Clog-Dance Costume

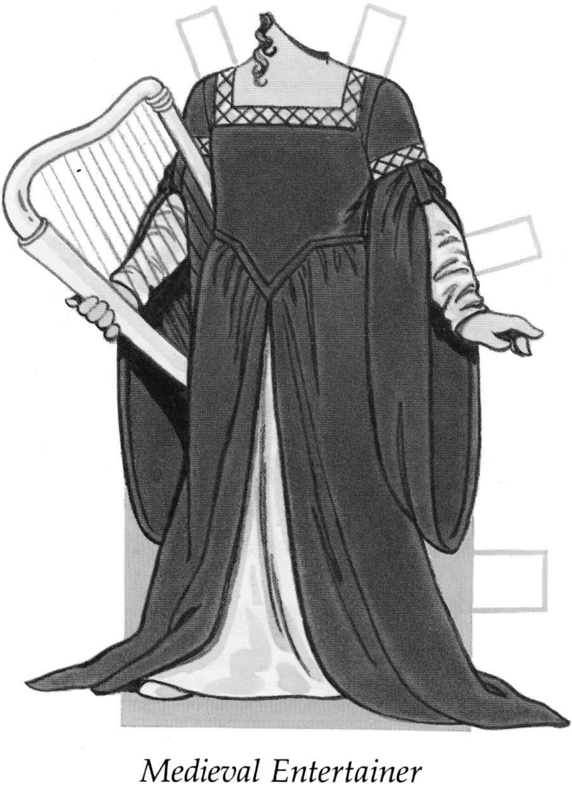

Medieval Entertainer

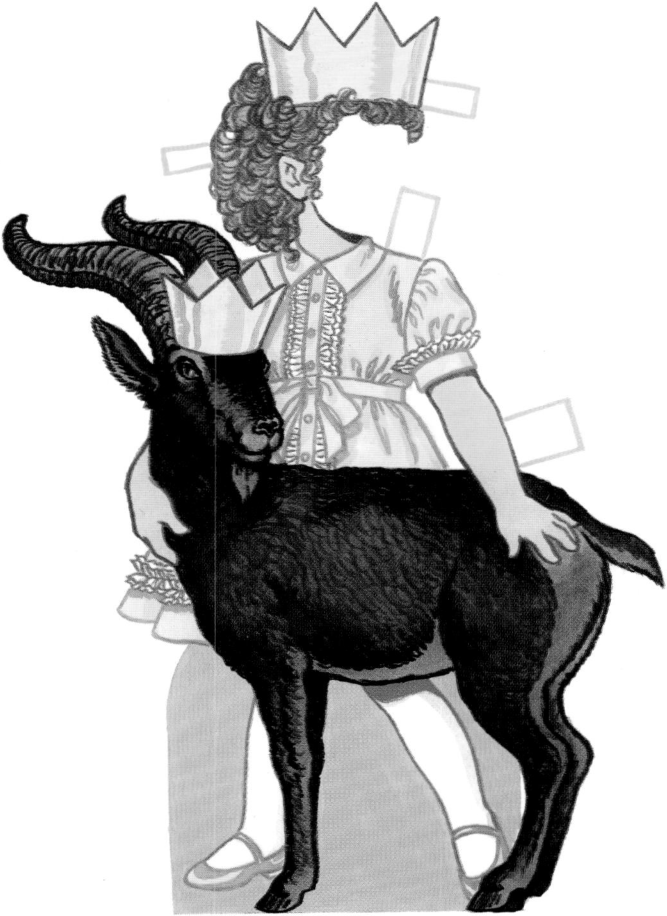

"Puck" Fair

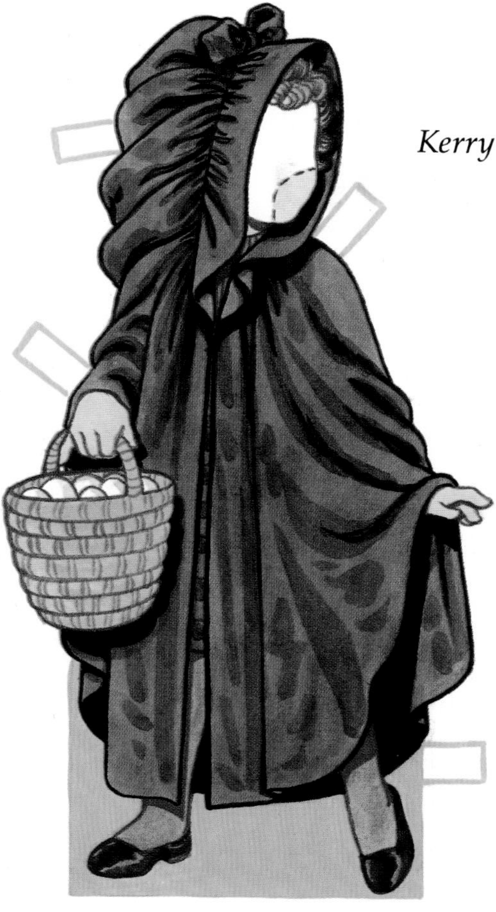

Kerry Cloak

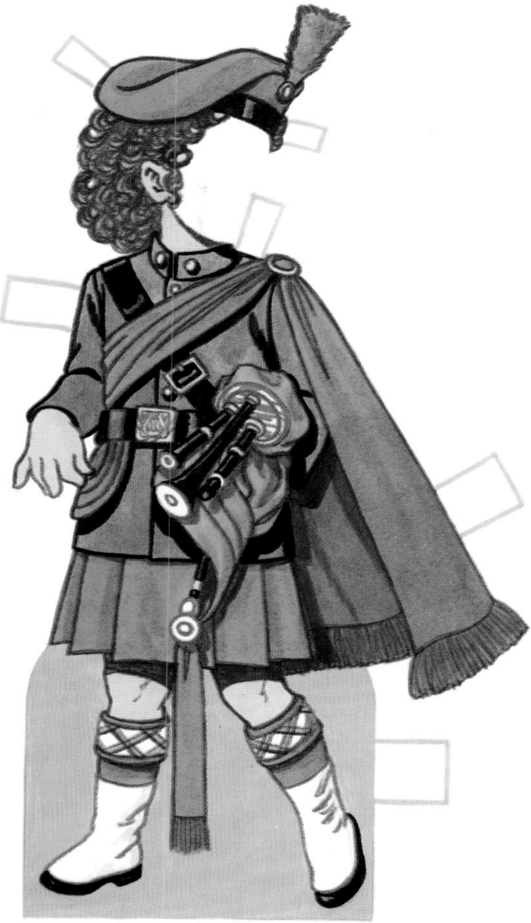

Kilt

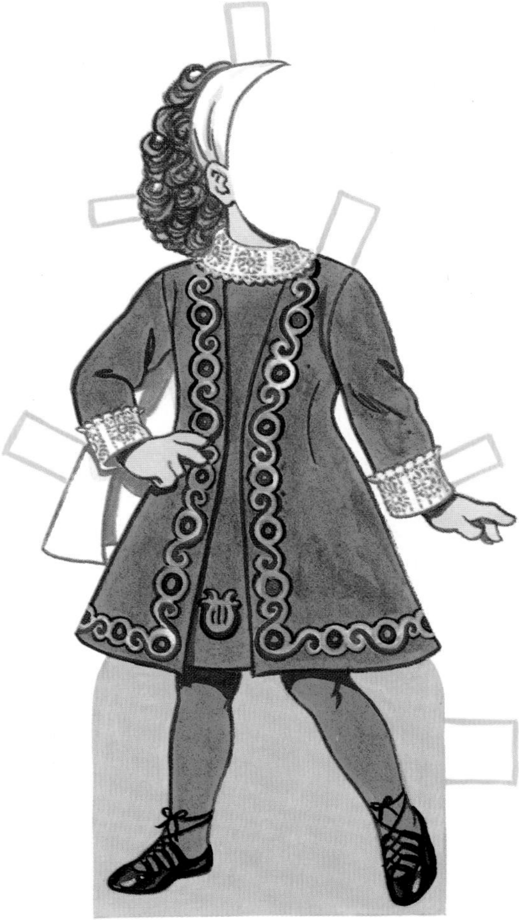

Step-Dance Costume

Knitted Shawl
from the Aran Islands

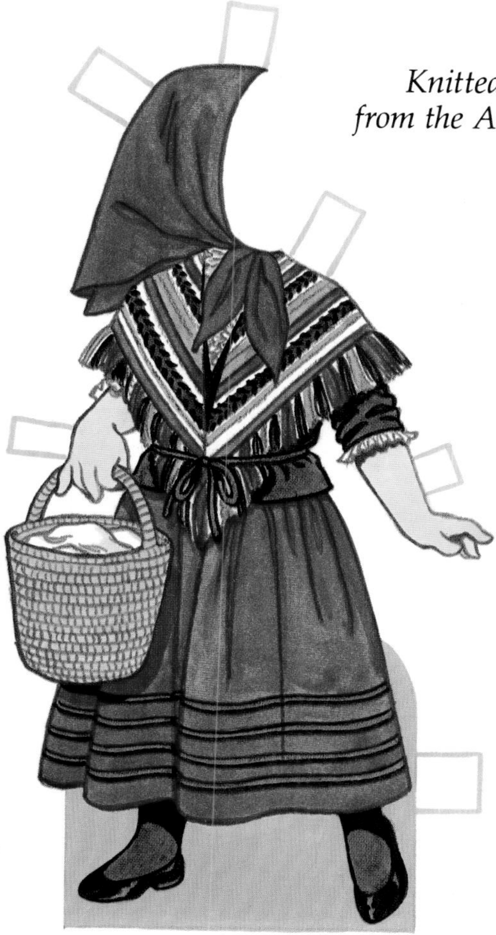

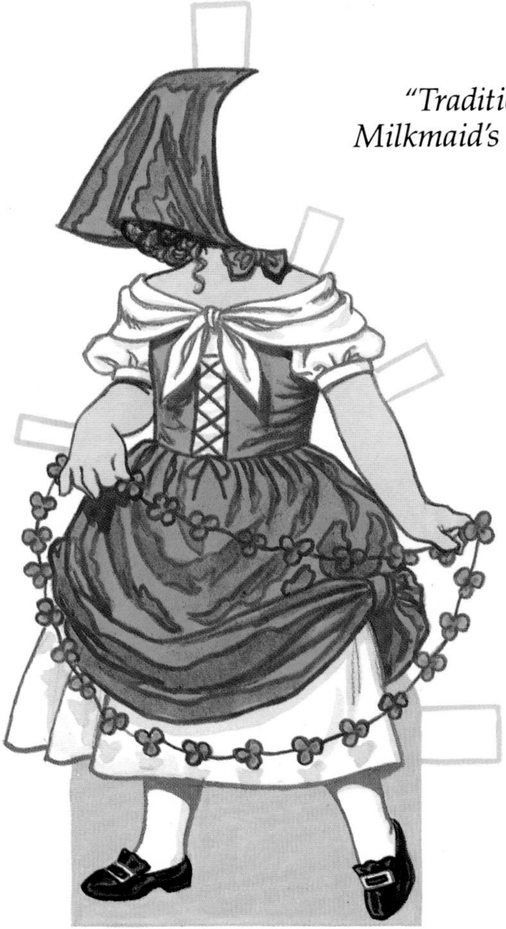

"Traditional" Milkmaid's Costume